Preamble:

In the vast expanse of Western Canada, a tale of transformation and leadership unfolds. It is a story of Queen Angela, a visionary ruler who defied conventions and embarked on a remarkable journey to reshape

he destiny of her beloved land. With unwavering determination and a deep understanding of the challenges that plagued the region, she set out on a path to unite the fragmented provinces and empower her people.

This is a tale that begins with the pursuit of truth. Western Alienation, a deeply rooted sentiment of disconnection and disillusionment, had plagued the region for far too long. Queen Angela, armed with the power of education and enlightenment, ventured to illuminate the hearts and minds of her people. She shattered misconceptions and unveiled the truth, instilling a sense of purpose and collective identity among the inhabitants of the West.

Through the power of knowledge, Queen Angela garnered the support of Alberta, the first province to join her cause. With each step, she navigated the intricate web of politics, incorporating British Columbia, Saskatchewan, and Manitoba into her coalition. The unity of the West grew stronger, fostering a shared vision for a prosperous and united region.

Yet, Queen Angela's ambitions knew no bounds. As her influence expanded, she sought to forge alliances beyond her borders. Ontario, a vital province in the east, recognized the wisdom and promise of her leadership, joining forces to shape a new era of collaboration and progress. With the foundation firmly laid in her homeland, Queen Angela set her sights on a more audacious goal—bringing her transformative power to the United States.

This is a saga of strategic diplomacy and audacious vision. It is a tale of economic resilience, environmental stewardship, social equity, and cultural pride. Through chapters that span continents and delve into the depths of human aspiration, we witness Queen Angela's unwavering dedication to her people and her unyielding pursuit of a brighter future.

Join us on this extraordinary journey, where the boundaries of possibility are pushed, and a ruler's legacy is forged. Explore the corridors of power, navigate the intricate dance of diplomacy, and witness the transformative power of leadership. The tale of Queen Angela and her quest to reshape Western Canada and beyond awaits, inviting you to be a part of this remarkable narrative.

Chapter 1: A Divided Nation

Queen Angela stood atop a podium, facing a sea of eager faces in Alberta. Her voice carried with conviction as she spoke about the injustices and grievances faced by the Western provinces. She painted a vivid picture of a nation divided, highlighting the sense of alienation that had plagued the region for far too long.

Chapter 2: Awakening the West

Queen Angela embarked on a tireless mission to educate the population of Alberta about Western Alienation. She held town hall meetings, engaged in one-on-one conversations, and organized grassroots movements. Her message resonated deeply with the people as they recognized her genuine concern and unwavering determination.

Chapter 3: The Gathering Storm

News of Queen Angela's movement began to spread beyond Alberta's borders, catching the attention of the neighboring province, British Columbia. Word of her powerful speeches and unwavering commitment to Western unity inspired the people of British Columbia to join the cause. The seeds of change were sown.

Chapter 4: Uniting the West

Queen Angela's influence continued to grow as she journeyed to Saskatchewan and Manitoba. She tirelessly traveled from town to town, speaking to crowds of citizens hungry for change. Her words stirred hope and unity among the people, as they recognized that together they could overcome the challenges they faced.

Chapter 5: Seeds of Doubt

As Queen Angela's movement gained momentum, opposition and skepticism arose from those who had benefited from the status quo. Political rivals and vested interests sought to undermine her message, spreading doubt and fear. Yet, Queen Angela remained steadfast, believing in the power of education and dialogue to overcome these obstacles.

Chapter 6: Forging Alliances

Recognizing the importance of political support, Queen Angela began to form alliances with like-minded individuals and groups. She sought out influential leaders, activists, and organizations who shared her vision for a united West. Together, they would amplify their voices and build a formidable coalition.

Chapter 7: Challenging the Status Quo

Queen Angela's movement faced its first major test as it encountered resistance from the entrenched political establishment. Her calls for change and unity challenged the existing power structures and sparked intense debates. The battle for hearts and minds intensified, and Queen Angela remained resolute in the face of adversity.

Chapter 8: Unmasking the Truth

Queen Angela launched an extensive campaign to expose the truth about Western Alienation. She engaged in public debates, televised interviews, and social media campaigns. Her team meticulously gathered data, facts, and personal stories to dismantle the misconceptions and reveal the real struggles faced by the West.

Chapter 9: Building Bridges

Queen Angela turned her attention to Ontario, a key province in the Canadian landscape. Recognizing the need for unity, she sought to bridge the divide between the East and the West. She embarked on a diplomatic journey, meeting with influential leaders and highlighting the shared values and aspirations between the two regions.

Chapter 10: Ontario's Awakening

Queen Angela's message resonated deeply with the people of Ontario, who had long been disillusioned with the centralized power of the nation's capital. They saw in Queen Angela a champion for their own concerns and a leader who could bridge the gap between the East and the West. Ontario joined the growing movement, further strengthening Queen Angela's cause.

With the first ten chapters set, the stage is now set for Queen Angela's journey to incorporate the Western provinces, gain support from Ontario, and ultimately expand her power to the United States. The story will continue to explore the challenges, triumphs, and transformative impact of her visionary leadership.

Chapter 11: A Coalition of the Willing

Queen Angela and her growing coalition of Western provinces and Ontario faced a critical juncture. They knew that to effect real change, they needed a united front. In this chapter, Queen Angela convened a summit of leaders from Alberta, British Columbia, Saskatchewan, Manitoba, and Ontario. Together, they forged a formal alliance, pledging to work collaboratively to address the issues of Western Alienation and promote regional interests. The coalition marked a turning point, as the power of unity became a force to be reckoned with.

Chapter 12: The Battle for Recognition

Armed with a formidable alliance, Queen Angela and her coalition turned their attention to the rest of Canada. In this chapter, they embarked on a strategic campaign to raise awareness and gain recognition for their cause. Queen Angela delivered impassioned speeches across the country, emphasizing the importance of inclusivity and acknowledging the unique challenges faced by the Western provinces. The battle for recognition began in earnest, as they sought to shift the national narrative and secure a seat at the table.

Chapter 13: Seeds of Doubt

As Queen Angela's movement gained traction, opposition from entrenched interests and political rivals intensified. In this chapter, Queen Angela and her coalition faced a barrage of attacks, smear campaigns, and attempts to delegitimize their message. They weathered the storm, remaining steadfast in their pursuit of justice and unity. Queen Angela's resilience inspired her supporters and exposed the desperation of those threatened by change.

Chapter 14: The Journey to Ottawa

The time had come for Queen Angela and her coalition to take their message directly to the nation's capital. In this chapter, they orchestrated a historic march on Ottawa, drawing attention from media outlets across the country. Thousands of supporters descended upon Parliament Hill, demanding that their voices be heard. Queen Angela delivered a rousing speech, challenging the status quo and calling for a more equitable and unified Canada.

Chapter 15: The Turning Tide

The march on Ottawa proved to be a pivotal moment. The impact of Queen Angela's message and the overwhelming support from the public began to sway opinion across the country. In this chapter, prominent figures from various provinces publicly voiced their support for the coalition's goals. The turning tide of public opinion placed pressure on the federal government to address Western Alienation and engage in meaningful dialogue.

Chapter 16: Negotiating the New Frontier

With momentum on their side, Queen Angela and her coalition entered into negotiations with the federal government. In this chapter, they advocated for greater autonomy, increased representation, and fairer distribution of resources for the Western provinces. Queen Angela's diplomacy and negotiation skills were put to the test as she navigated the complexities of forging a new frontier of cooperation within the Canadian federation.

Chapter 17: Securing Progress

As negotiations progressed, Queen Angela and her coalition secured significant wins. In this chapter, they achieved key policy reforms, including increased infrastructure investment in the West, the establishment of regional decision-making bodies, and greater recognition of Western perspectives in national policies. These victories solidified the coalition's standing and showcased the power of collaboration and determination.

Chapter 18: The United States Connection

Queen Angela's vision extended beyond Canada's borders. In this chapter, she set her sights on strengthening ties with the United States. Recognizing the economic and geopolitical advantages of a strong partnership, she embarked on a diplomatic mission southward. Through trade agreements, cultural exchanges, and shared initiatives, Queen Angela sought to forge a deeper connection between Western Canada and its southern neighbor.

Chapter 19: A Fragile Balance

As Queen Angela expanded her influence, she faced a delicate balancing act. In this chapter, tensions arose within the coalition as differing priorities and regional interests came to the forefront. Queen Angela worked tirelessly to maintain unity and ensure that the collective vision remained intact. Compromises were made, alliances were strengthened, and the delicate balance of power was preserved.

Chapter 20: Shifting Dynamics

The success of Queen Angela's coalition and her ability to effect change began to reshape the political landscape. In this chapter, traditional party lines blurred as politicians from various parties rallied behind the cause of Western unity. The old divisions were replaced by a new political landscape where regional interests gained prominence. Queen Angela's movement had sparked a seismic shift in the dynamics of Canadian politics.

With these chapters, the narrative of Queen Angela's quest to unite Western Canada and expand her power to the United States gains further depth and complexity. The story continues to explore the challenges, triumphs, and evolving dynamics of her visionary leadership.

Chapter 21: The Crossroads of Change

Queen Angela found herself at a critical crossroads. In this chapter, she grappled with the decision of whether to pursue a more assertive approach in her quest to bring the United States into her fold or to focus on consolidating her achievements within Canada. Consulting with her trusted advisors, she weighed the potential risks and rewards of each path, knowing that the choices she made would have far-reaching consequences.

Chapter 22: A Transcontinental Alliance

Opting for a bold approach, Queen Angela initiated a series of high-level talks with American leaders. In this chapter, she sought to forge a transcontinental alliance that would deepen economic integration, foster cultural exchange, and enhance regional cooperation. The negotiations were complex, with both countries carefully considering the benefits and potential challenges of such a partnership.

Chapter 23: Bridging the Divide

Queen Angela's efforts to bridge the divide between Canada and the United States faced initial skepticism and resistance. In this chapter, she embarked on a diplomatic tour, visiting key cities and engaging with influential figures on both sides of the border. Through public addresses and private meetings, Queen Angela emphasized the shared values, common interests, and mutual benefits of a closer relationship.

Chapter 24: Overcoming Hurdles

As the negotiations progressed, Queen Angela encountered several hurdles along the way. This chapter delves into the various obstacles she faced, including differences in political systems, trade regulations, and cultural sensitivities. Queen Angela's determination and adept negotiation skills were put to the test as she worked tirelessly to overcome these challenges and pave the way for a transformative alliance.

Chapter 25: The Treaty of Unity

Amidst intense negotiations, Queen Angela and the United States reached a breakthrough. In this chapter, they finalized the Treaty of Unity, a landmark agreement that laid the foundation for a deepened partnership between the two nations. The treaty encompassed economic cooperation, defense alliances, environmental initiatives, and cultural exchanges, marking a historic milestone in Queen Angela's ambitious plan.

Chapter 26: Public Opinion and Opposition

The announcement of the Treaty of Unity sparked a wide range of reactions. This chapter explores the public sentiment and the varying degrees of support and opposition to the alliance. Queen Angela faced fierce criticism from those wary of relinquishing Canadian sovereignty and concerned about the potential consequences of such a transformative agreement. She navigated these challenges, engaging in dialogue, and addressing the legitimate concerns raised by her fellow citizens.

Chapter 27: Implementing the Alliance

With the treaty in place, the real work of implementing the alliance began. In this chapter, Queen Angela and her team focused on coordinating efforts, aligning policies, and establishing joint initiatives that would strengthen the bond between the two nations. Collaborative projects in trade, security, research, and cultural exchange were initiated, laying the groundwork for a deep and lasting partnership.

Chapter 28: A Changing Landscape

The impact of the alliance between Western Canada and the United States began to reshape the geopolitical landscape. This chapter explores how the newfound unity influenced global perceptions and international relations. Queen Angela's visionary leadership and her ability to forge such a strategic alliance elevated Western Canada's standing on the world stage, leading to increased opportunities and influence in global affairs.

Chapter 29: Unity Tested

As the alliance progressed, it faced its fair share of tests and challenges. This chapter delves into the internal and external pressures that threatened to strain the unity between Western Canada and the United States. Queen Angela and her counterparts on both sides of the border had to navigate disagreements, economic fluctuations, and geopolitical complexities while maintaining the spirit of collaboration and shared goals.

Chapter 30: Advancing Together

Despite the obstacles, Queen Angela's alliance with the United States continued to evolve. In this chapter, we witness the joint achievements and progress made in various sectors.

Economic ties deepened, technological advancements were shared, and cultural exchanges flourished. Queen Angela's visionary leadership and her ability to navigate the complexities of international relations solidified the alliance's foundations and propelled both nations forward.

With these chapters, the narrative expands to explore the intricacies and challenges of Queen Angela's pursuit to bring the United States into her fold. The story continues to unravel the transformative impact of her leadership and the evolving dynamics between Western Canada and its newfound partner.

Chapter 31: Strains and Struggles

Queen Angela faced growing tensions within her coalition and the challenges of maintaining unity. In this chapter, differing regional interests and political ambitions threatened to strain the alliance she had worked so hard to build. Queen Angela engaged in intense negotiations, seeking compromises and solutions to ensure the cohesion and effectiveness of her coalition.

Chapter 32: Navigating International Relations

As the alliance between Western Canada and the United States gained prominence, Queen

Angela found herself navigating the complex web of international relations. In this chapter, she attended global summits, engaged in diplomatic negotiations, and forged partnerships with other nations. Queen Angela's ability to balance the interests of her coalition while pursuing global cooperation proved crucial in shaping Western Canada's position on the international stage.

Chapter 33: Environmental Imperatives

Recognizing the urgent need to address environmental challenges, Queen Angela placed a strong emphasis on sustainability and conservation. In this chapter, she implemented ambitious environmental policies, promoting renewable energy initiatives, and advocating for responsible resource management. Queen Angela's commitment to protecting the environment resonated with the public, solidifying her position as a leader dedicated to the long-term well-being of the region.

Chapter 34: Cultural Exchanges

Cultural exchanges played a pivotal role in fostering understanding and appreciation between Western Canada and the United States. This chapter explores the diverse range of initiatives undertaken to promote cultural exchange, including art exhibitions, music festivals, and educational programs. Queen Angela understood the importance of bridging cultural divides and nurturing a sense of shared identity among the people of both nations.

Chapter 35: Securing Borders

As the alliance between Western Canada and the United States deepened, securing the borders became a paramount concern. In this chapter, Queen Angela led efforts to enhance border security measures while maintaining the smooth flow of trade and travel. Collaborative intelligence sharing, joint law enforcement operations, and streamlined border procedures were implemented to ensure the safety and prosperity of both nations.

Chapter 36: Economic Integration

Economic integration between Western Canada and the United States flourished under Queen Angela's leadership. This chapter explores the transformative impact of trade agreements, investment partnerships, and joint economic ventures. Queen Angela's focus on fostering innovation, attracting foreign investment, and creating opportunities for businesses fueled economic growth and prosperity on both sides of the border.

Chapter 37: Educational Empowerment

Queen Angela recognized that education was a cornerstone of progress and empowerment. In this chapter, she spearheaded initiatives to improve educational systems, expand access to quality education, and promote research collaboration. Queen Angela's commitment to nurturing the intellectual potential of her people laid the groundwork for a more innovative and knowledge-driven society.

Chapter 38: The Quest for Reconciliation

Queen Angela embarked on a journey of reconciliation with indigenous communities. This chapter delves into her efforts to address historical injustices, promote cultural preservation, and foster meaningful partnerships with indigenous peoples. Queen Angela's dedication to reconciliation and her commitment to acknowledging the rights and contributions of indigenous communities strengthened the social fabric of Western Canada.

Chapter 39: Technological Advancements

Queen Angela championed technological advancements and innovation as drivers of progress. In this chapter, she implemented policies to foster research and development, attract tech startups, and invest in digital infrastructure. Queen Angela's vision for a technologically advanced Western Canada positioned the region as a hub of innovation and created new opportunities for economic growth and societal advancement.

Chapter 40: Crisis Management

Queen Angela faced her first major crisis as a leader. This chapter explores how she handled a significant natural disaster that threatened both Western Canada and the United States. Queen Angela demonstrated decisive leadership, mobilizing resources, coordinating relief efforts, and providing support to affected communities. Her ability to effectively manage the crisis and rally the collective strength of the alliance showcased her resilience and unwavering commitment to the well-being of her people.

These chapters delve into the complexities of Queen Angela's leadership as she navigates internal and external challenges, fosters collaboration, and propels Western Canada's progress in various spheres. The narrative continues to evolve, showcasing the breadth of Queen Angela's vision and the transformative impact of her governance.

Chapter 41: Trade Diplomacy

Queen Angela focused on expanding trade relations beyond North America. In this chapter, she embarked on a series of diplomatic missions to strengthen economic ties with countries around the world. Queen Angela negotiated trade agreements, facilitated investment opportunities, and promoted Western Canada's export industries. These efforts opened up new markets and avenues for growth, bolstering the region's economic prosperity.

Chapter 42: A New Energy Frontier

Queen Angela recognized the importance of transitioning to a sustainable energy future. In this chapter, she spearheaded initiatives to promote renewable energy sources, reduce carbon emissions, and invest in clean technologies. Queen Angela's commitment to environmental stewardship and innovation propelled Western Canada to the forefront of the global clean energy revolution.

Chapter 43: Defending Regional Interests

As Western Canada's influence grew, so did the need to protect its regional interests. In this chapter, Queen Angela navigated geopolitical challenges and defended the rights and aspirations of her coalition. She engaged in strategic alliances, fostered diplomatic relationships, and ensured Western Canada's voice was heard on the international stage. Queen Angela's determination to safeguard regional autonomy strengthened Western Canada's position in the global arena.

Chapter 44: Strengthening Infrastructure

Recognizing the importance of robust infrastructure for economic growth, Queen Angela prioritized infrastructure development. In this chapter, she spearheaded ambitious projects to enhance transportation networks, build sustainable cities, and improve connectivity within and beyond Western Canada. Queen Angela's vision for modern and efficient infrastructure laid the foundation for increased productivity, improved quality of life, and enhanced regional integration.

Chapter 45: Cultural Renaissance

Under Queen Angela's leadership, Western Canada experienced a cultural renaissance. This chapter explores the flourishing arts scene, with vibrant festivals, thriving theaters, and dynamic creative industries. Queen Angela's support for cultural expression and investment in artistic endeavors revitalized Western Canada's cultural identity, fostering a sense of pride and creativity among its diverse communities.

Chapter 46: Health and Well-being

Queen Angela prioritized the health and well-being of her people. In this chapter, she implemented comprehensive healthcare reforms, focused on preventive care, and promoted mental health initiatives. Queen Angela's commitment to accessible and quality healthcare ensured that the people of Western Canada enjoyed a high standard of living and holistic support for their well-being.

Chapter 47: Harnessing Indigenous Wisdom

Queen Angela continued her journey of reconciliation and collaboration with indigenous communities. In this chapter, she recognized the importance of indigenous knowledge and wisdom in shaping sustainable policies and practices. Queen Angela fostered partnerships with indigenous leaders, engaging them in decision-making processes and integrating their perspectives into governance and resource management.

Chapter 48: Scientific Advancements

Queen Angela emphasized scientific research and innovation as drivers of progress. In this chapter, she bolstered funding for research institutions, encouraged cross-disciplinary collaboration, and attracted leading scientists and thinkers to Western Canada. Queen Angela's investment in scientific advancements propelled the region to the forefront of technological breakthroughs, driving economic growth and societal transformation.

Chapter 49: Crisis of Confidence

Queen Angela faced a crisis of confidence within her coalition. In this chapter, disagreements and conflicting interests strained the unity she had worked so hard to maintain. Queen Angela sought to bridge the gaps, engaging in open dialogue, and reassessing policies to address the concerns of her coalition members. Her unwavering determination to find common ground and restore trust tested her leadership skills.

Chapter 50: A Vision Realized

Queen Angela's relentless pursuit of unity and progress reached a critical juncture. In this chapter, she reflected on the milestones achieved, the challenges overcome, and the collective journey of Western Canada. Queen Angela's vision for a prosperous, inclusive, and influential Western Canada had become a reality. Her transformative leadership and unwavering commitment to her people's well-being left an indelible mark on the region's history.

With these chapters, the narrative deepens the exploration of Queen Angela's governance as she expands trade, fosters cultural and environmental renaissance, strengthens infrastructure, and navigates challenges and crises. The story continues to unfold, showcasing the complexities and triumphs of Queen Angela's quest to realize her vision for Western Canada.

Chapter 51: Technological Diplomacy

Queen Angela recognized the power of technological diplomacy in shaping international relations. In this chapter, she leveraged Western Canada's technological advancements to forge strategic partnerships with nations around the world. Through collaborative research, knowledge exchange, and joint innovation projects, Queen Angela solidified Western Canada's position as a global hub of technological excellence.

Chapter 52: Strengthening Education Systems

Queen Angela placed a strong emphasis on strengthening education systems. In this chapter, she implemented reforms to enhance curriculum standards, promote inclusivity, and invest in educational infrastructure. Queen Angela's commitment to providing quality education for all fostered a highly skilled workforce, nurtured talent, and fueled innovation and economic growth throughout Western Canada.

Chapter 53: Balancing Growth and Sustainability

Queen Angela faced the delicate task of balancing economic growth with environmental sustainability. In this chapter, she implemented policies to ensure responsible resource development, promote sustainable practices in industries, and protect fragile ecosystems. Queen Angela's commitment to achieving a harmonious balance between economic prosperity and environmental stewardship set Western Canada as a global model for sustainable development.

Chapter 54: Diplomatic Challenges

As Western Canada's influence grew on the global stage, Queen Angela encountered diplomatic challenges. This chapter delves into the complexities of international relations, navigating geopolitical rivalries, and addressing contentious issues. Queen Angela's diplomatic finesse, strategic alliances, and commitment to multilateral cooperation enabled her to overcome obstacles and advance Western Canada's interests on the world stage.

Chapter 55: Social Equity and Inclusion

Queen Angela prioritized social equity and inclusion as cornerstones of her governance. In this chapter, she championed policies to address inequality, promote diversity, and empower marginalized communities. Queen Angela's commitment to social justice created a more inclusive society where all individuals had equal opportunities to thrive and contribute to Western Canada's progress.

Chapter 56: Strengthening National Identity

As Western Canada's influence grew, Queen Angela focused on strengthening the region's national identity. In this chapter, she celebrated Western Canada's unique cultural heritage, promoted national symbols, and fostered a sense of pride and unity among its people. Queen Angela's efforts to shape a distinct Western Canadian identity instilled a shared sense of purpose and belonging.

Chapter 57: Innovation Hubs

Queen Angela envisioned Western Canada as a network of innovation hubs. In this chapter, she fostered the growth of technology clusters, research centers, and startup incubators across the region. Queen Angela's investment in innovation infrastructure and supportive policies attracted talent, spurred entrepreneurship, and propelled Western Canada to the forefront of technological advancements.

Chapter 58: Climate Leadership

Queen Angela positioned Western Canada as a global leader in climate action. In this chapter, she implemented ambitious carbon reduction targets, encouraged renewable energy adoption, and mobilized efforts to mitigate the impacts of climate change. Queen Angela's commitment to climate leadership earned Western Canada international acclaim and positioned the region as a driving force in global environmental sustainability.

Chapter 59: Securing Future Generations

Queen Angela focused on securing a prosperous future for the next generations. In this chapter, she implemented policies to support youth empowerment, expand access to education and healthcare, and create opportunities for personal and professional growth. Queen Angela's dedication to investing in the well-being and success of future generations cemented Western Canada's legacy as a region that prioritized intergenerational equity.

Chapter 60: Economic Resilience

Queen Angela faced economic challenges that tested Western Canada's resilience. In this chapter, she implemented strategies to diversify the economy, reduce dependence on specific industries, and promote entrepreneurship and innovation. Queen Angela's foresight and proactive measures ensured that Western Canada remained adaptable, competitive, and resilient in the face of economic fluctuations and global uncertainties.

These chapters deepen the exploration of Queen Angela's governance, addressing technological diplomacy, education, sustainability, social equity, national identity, innovation, climate leadership, intergenerational equity, and economic resilience. The story continues to unfold, highlighting the multifaceted nature of Queen Angela's leadership and her enduring commitment to shaping Western Canada's future.

Chapter 61: Cross-Border Collaboration

Queen Angela turned her attention to strengthening cross-border collaboration with neighboring regions and countries. In this chapter, she engaged in diplomatic efforts to foster cooperation on issues of mutual interest, such as trade, security, and environmental conservation. Queen Angela's commitment to cross-border collaboration fostered peace, stability, and shared prosperity in the region.

Chapter 62: Global Humanitarian Initiatives

Queen Angela championed global humanitarian initiatives as part of Western Canada's foreign policy. In this chapter, she led efforts to provide aid and support to countries facing humanitarian crises, whether due to natural disasters or conflicts. Queen Angela's compassion and commitment to global solidarity earned Western Canada a reputation as a reliable and compassionate international partner.

Chapter 63: Art and Cultural Diplomacy

Recognizing the power of art and culture in fostering understanding and forging connections, Queen Angela focused on art and cultural diplomacy. In this chapter, she promoted cultural exchanges, organized international arts festivals, and supported artists from Western Canada on the global stage. Queen Angela's dedication to art and cultural diplomacy enhanced Western Canada's soft power and deepened international appreciation for its rich cultural heritage.

Chapter 64: Sustainable Urban Development

Queen Angela prioritized sustainable urban development as cities in Western Canada continued to grow. In this chapter, she implemented policies to promote eco-friendly infrastructure, walkability, and public transportation systems. Queen Angela's vision for sustainable urbanization created livable, vibrant cities that balanced economic growth with environmental preservation, enhancing the quality of life for Western Canada's urban dwellers.

Chapter 65: The Global Stage

Queen Angela's leadership propelled Western Canada onto the global stage. In this chapter, she participated in international summits, represented Western Canada in global organizations, and advocated for the region's interests on the world stage. Queen Angela's presence and influence on the global stage elevated Western Canada's profile, enabling it to contribute meaningfully to global discussions and shape international agendas.

These chapters highlight Queen Angela's efforts to foster cross-border collaboration, engage in global humanitarian initiatives, utilize art and cultural diplomacy, promote sustainable urban development, and navigate the complexities of international relations. Queen Angela's leadership continues to expand Western Canada's influence and pave the way for a more interconnected and sustainable world.

www.ingramcontent.com/pod-product-compliance
Lightning Source LLC
Chambersburg PA
CBHW060908260726
48661CB00008B/3536